MW01227235

PRANA

A Therapeutic Guide to Pranayama

Ramesh Mishra

TABLE OF CONTENTS

INTRODUCTION

The Kundalini is an enthusiastic pathway in the body that runs from the base of your spine up along your spine, up the rear of your take and off the highest point of your head.

There are numerous enthusiastic pathways in the body, yet there are two primary vitality pathways. One climbs the focal point of the front of the body and the Kundalini, which runs up the focal point of the rear of the casing.

In otherworldly practices, for example, contemplation, you are expanding the measure of vitality (otherwise called Kundalini Shakti) that travels through these channels. The force itself starts to clean and broaden these vitality channels with the goal that more Kundalini Shakti can walkthrough. The more vitality, the more profound your mindfulness and happiness.

Some numerous strategies and practices are utilized to expand the Kundalini Shakti with the goal that an otherworldly arousing or Kundalini arousing can happen. One strategy is through the breath.

A basic breathing strategy that can help stir the Kundalini is to close your eyes, sit upright and inhale up your spine.

Start by concentrating on the base of your spine and as you breathe in to move your consideration up along your spine and out the highest point of your head (following the pathway of the Kundalini). At that point, as you breathe out to move your concentration from the highest point of your head down the front focus of your brow, face, throat and afterwards let the breath out the end at the focal point of your chest.

Rehash the procedure, beginning again at the base of your spine.

Right now every breath, you are moving your consideration in a fractional hover; beginning at top base of your spine up along your spine and out the highest point of your head and afterwards down through your third eye, throat and afterwards your heart at the focal point of your chest.

A fundamental part to arousing your Kundalini is to get Kundalini Shakti. By only accepting Kundalini Shakti, your Kundalini and other vigorous pathways normally become stirred.

At the point when you get Kundalini Shakti, you normally feel it as unlimited harmony, ecstasy or love. On point the most straightforward approach to stir your Kundalini is to focus on this sentiment of satisfaction as it were. The more you stay mindful and permitting of this ecstasy, the more the delight increments. The essential method to getting Kundalini Shakti is to sit with a completely edified ace of contemplation. An altogether proficient educator normally transmits Shakti.

CHAPTER ONE
KUNDALINI AWAKENING

Before we talk about kundalini stimulating, we need to fathom the significance of kundalini! The kundalini Shakti is that covered constructive imperativeness set aside in every individual by stimulating which every individual can land at the level of Mahavira, Gautama Buddha, Jesus Christ and Prophet Mohammed.

The animating of the kundalini is possible by practicing the right Yoga and examination. In the common conditions, the animating of the kundalini ought to happen inside a period of 11 million appearances as a person. A veritable searcher of extraordinary quality reliably needs Kundalini exciting at the soonest.

Each undeniable searcher of supernatural quality appreciates that aside from if the kundalini stimulating occurs... one won't have the choice to land at the level of Nirvikalpa

Samadhi and the period of self-affirmation. Kundalini stirring is a hundred per cent ought to before one can get enlightenment right now.

Kundalini is the concentrated imperativeness of care or thought. It isn't imperativeness isolated from mindfulness, yet rather the essentialness that demonstrates with discernment when it ends up being liberated from thought." That is the explanation a gave examination practice can engage kundalini to stream, as the discontinuance of contemplations is a target of explicit sorts of reflection while in transit to solidarity.

Kara-Leah Grant explains, "When Kundalini blends, an individual may experience further empathy with others, and this compassion can almost wind up perceptive. There is progressively imperative affectability, higher essentialness levels, every so often spiritualist limits or significant knowing, developing can appear to chill out, creativity and attraction can augment, as can inside the agreement and knowing. There is an inclination of being a bit of All that Is. The more critical insider facts of life are never again questions."

A person that recognizes significant illumination through a kundalini stirring may work in the repairing articulations. They tend to work in agreeableness with their genuine life's calling, perhaps hailing a distinction in callings. They may lose excitement for material things while winding up dynamically liberal. They may talk less and picked words with increasingly significant clarity and significance.

In the clearest terms, a Kundalini Awakening is a strategy for exploiting a significant and mind-blowing sort of imperativeness that exists inside us all. This imperativeness would then have the option to be used to expand increasingly essential information, improving your understanding or yourself just as others. A couple of experts depict Kundalini simply like the specific sort of imperativeness that shows in our discerning characters when we free ourselves from perceptive thought.

What might you have the option to expect when you experience a Kundalini Awakening? This is a noteworthy move that improves sympathy, gives you all around sharpened natural judgment, and empowers you to find a level of assurance you've at no other time experienced. These movements help you to not simply separate what you truly need from your life yet moreover to look for after those goals. In case there are things you've recently ached for doing however never genuinely endeavoured to appear, a Kundalini Awakening could be the strategy that pushes those dreams past inventive personality and into this present reality.

Stacks of "reactions" get denounced on kundalini – from muscle fits to seeing tones strikingly to not having the alternative to rest.

In my view, it's not just the kundalini imperativeness that is causing unsafe reactions, anyway the physical, enthusiastic and mental blockages that are not empowering that essentialness to stream. Kundalini imperativeness is just the central intensity of life, the essentialness of care that exists in each and every one of us. Right when we experience kundalini "appearances", that essentialness is pounding on the passage to stand sufficiently apart to be seen and care so we can turn out positive enhancements. Exactly when that happens, we can advance toward turning out to be what our personality is planned to be and wake up to our destiny.

The soul has taken a body and come here for clarification, and in case you have not encountered that reason, kundalini can show up as dangerous so you can change course. It's an (at times not too fragile) update with the objective that we don't sleepwalk through life.

HISTORY OF KUNDALINI

But a noteworthy piece of the verifiable setting of Kundalini related practices is dark, and there is some verification that notice has been made of the essentialness power in various out of date works. Found in works from the Tibetans, Chinese, Egyptians, and Native Americans, there is furthermore reference to this sort of force in the Bible and the Koran. In spite of the way that most social orders didn't clearly practice Kundalini Yoga or exciting sessions, it ended up being even more extensively known through created via Carl Jung during the 1930s.

During the 1970s, people in general wound up enthralled with the demonstration of Kundalini Yoga and began searching for finding out about the preparation. The 70s were a time of fantastic powerful stirring wherever all through the world, it is the description such a noteworthy number of people began to practice yoga and other significantly genuine experiences. Nevertheless, that there are various sorts of yoga, not which are altogether dedicated to emerging the Kundalini, it was one of the various unmistakable practice right now.

Over the latest 150 years, two individuals have viably mixed their kundalini and recognized God. Sri Ramakrishna Paramhansa and Maharishi Ramana while proceeding in transit of unadulterated, powerful nature searching for God had their kundalini mixed totally. It was basically after their kundalini had mixed were they prepared to land at the period of Nirvikalpa samadhi.

Each conspicuous searcher of powerful nature grasps the criticalness of kundalini stimulating. In case we are to recognize God inside our lifetime, we have to mix our kundalini totally right now. But in the event that we take the lift straight up, we won't land at the level of a mixed one, a living Buddha!

Kundalini stimulating, in any case, frightful it may have all the earmarks of being, is illustrative of the positive powers of the Cosmos overpowering the underhanded forces until the finish of time.

Every God recognized soul lands at the level of a Mahavira, Gautama Buddha, Jesus Christ or Prophet Mohammed basically in the wake of having vanquished the negative forces forever by stirring of the kundalini.

Kundalini stimulating is better possible in a Man. The prime inspiration driving why in the whole history of mankind, only two ladies had their kundalini mixed totally. Gargi, the solitary officer researcher and Maitreyi, the notable companion of Sage Jnanavalakya!

Gargi was that special lady who has blended her kundalini engaged herself with the notable trades with Pundit Mandan Mishra regarding the matter of sex. Gargi finally squashed Pundit Mandan Mishra for she was a real God recognized soul. Academic Mandan Mishra still couldn't appear to mix his kundalini.

Sage Jnanavalakya was that staggering force in the long stretches of ruler Janaka that even before the test among 10,000 savvy people and sages amassed before a crowd of people had begun... Sage Jnanavalakya mentioned the prize money to be brought home. Sage Jnanavalakya was a truly God recognized soul. His kundalini had mixed totally, and he understood that none in the get-together had landed at his level of extraordinary satisfaction.

Kundalini symptoms are a trademark reaction when people mix the kundalini in their body and cerebrum. The word 'kundalini' starts from the Hindu show and is used to depict a kind of mysterious imperativeness that misrepresentations dormant in every single one of us at the foot of our spine. Right when mixed this essentialness climbs the spine, refines all chakras in transit until it lands at the head where it gets together with its 'divine partner' and the individual lands at a light. Kundalini imperativeness has been delineated as hot, shuddering and awesome white essentialness.

EXPERIENCES OF KUNDALINI ALL OVER THE WORLD

The possibility of imperativeness from our stomach region rising to the head isn't compelled to Hinduism yet has been known in various extraordinary traditions wherever all through the world. In Tibetan Buddhism, it is called 'tummo' (really 'savage woman'), in parts of Taoism it is implied as 'neikung',, and in the Christian custom,, people have used explanations like 'the Essence of God went into him' or basically as 'magnificence'.

THE GIFTS OF KUNDALINI

All kundalini experiences share for all goals and reason that people feel basically overwhelmed by some unfathomable essentialness rushing through their structure and repaying them with bewildering powerful dreams, phenomenal satisfaction or favours like exceptional understanding or the ability to retouch others with the force of the mind. People may,, in like manner,, get surprising bits of information to questions that are basic to humankind, and theythey may have the choice to make certified works of art or help others in a noteworthy way. At the zenith of these experiences,, people may feel that they are getting together with God or finding a good pace.

THE CHALLENGES OF THE KUNDALINI AWAKENING

Deplorably, these sublime enrichments of kundalini stimulating are sometimes cultivated through one amazing,, and weighty accomplishment yet is the eventual outcome of various extensive stretches of working discreetly through the troubles that are the unavoidable reaction of even the most sympathetic kundalini rising. These signs of kundalini may run from confounding physical distress, to ridiculous eager disrupting impacts, up to anall-out crazy separate of one's working internal identity character. What fuels the circumstance, these unbearable experiences are ordinarily exacerbated by a lot of mental perplexitieses considering the way that the person who is encountering them often can't grasp what is happening to them.

Usually, it is told that kundalini rising (or anything people want to call it as shownby their social establishment) must be cultivated through extended lengths of dedicated powerful practice. Nevertheless, since the conveyance of Gopi Krishna's book 'Kundalini' various people have drawn nearer to report claimed unconstrained kundalini illuminations, which were liberated from genuine supernatural practice. During these unconstrained kundalini experiences as often as possible,, the negative and jumbling kundalini symptoms were significantly more explained than the repaying edges.

There are a wide scope of viewpoints on the Kundalini exciting procedure and moreover many fluctuating experiences. Some express that charging Kundalini can incite frenzy, others that it prompts illumination, that it is our legacyand the accompanying stage in human advancement. When Kundalini is blended,, it prompts an absurdity of sorts, lost one's mind, or mental self-portrait. As all of a marvellouss experiences return flooding to us and our care creates past anything we could have as of late imagined, it may feel like we are going insane, losing our mind, yet truth be told we are truly finding a good pace, breaking free from our formed, direct points of view, permitted to see reality with regards to and experience the universe. A huge move in our perspective occurs, and we become prepared to see the connectedness of all things and to comprehend our real nature and greatest limit.

As the methodology spreads out the outside layers of our selves are stripped away, a smidgen at once, until our real self ascents, away from all past karma and excited blockages. A change that happens from the back to front. Releasing and recovering any wounds that are so far being held inside the body and mindfulness. The inspiration driving why some are classed as insane or make mental issues is in light of the fact that they are endeavouring to stop or cover the methodology through traditional systems and without a real understanding of what's going on. Kundalini cleans the soul, the cerebrum and the physical body and it isn't startling to experience a kind of mental irritation and maybe physical agitating impact. Regardless, you should allow Kundalini to do what it needs to do, offer ready, don't set up the check as this will simply make the experience progressively unbalanced and horrendous. Make an effort not to fear it, welcome and bolster it, and the methodology will spread out in a fundamentally progressively friendly way. Addition capability with all that you can about Kundalini.

Look at differentiating points of view and make up your own one of a kind mind, find your own one of a kind truth. It's not possible for anyone to uncover to you what is right and what isn't, reality lays inside you, the learning is there starting at now, you just need to review.

There are certain techniques and frameworks which you can use yourself to mix Kundalini, including explicit sorts of examination and breathing strategies. Regardless, know, when you start on along these lines, there is no returning, as the people who mix Kundalini and after that endeavour to smother it will without a doubt experience issues. Some direction that Kundalini must be mixed by a 'Pro' or 'Ace', this is your choice and is completely dependent all alone level of Spiritual headway, singular data, appreciation and conviction system. If you endeavour and mix it yourself, by then, you should set up your mind and body for what is coming up, try to clear anyway numerous toxic substances from the body as could be permitted, eat well, and avoid alcohol and recreational prescriptions as these would all have the option to hamper the method and can incite issues. Keep dynamic, and you ought to find strategies for releasing excess imperativeness else it will wind up stale and could cause issues. An OK strategy to get physical activity together with the methodology is through Kundalini Yoga which was unequivocally made to mix Kundalini and is represented to be maybe the soonest sort of yoga. It resembles Hatha yoga yet with more focus on exciting Kundalini. Ha-tha really implies Sun-Moon, and yoga suggests affiliation, so a relationship of the sun and moon energies, which is what occurs during the Kundalini stirring procedure

OPENING THE THIRD EYE

One of the most sweeping blunders about stirring Kundalini is that it blends simultaneously and that the Third Eye opens absolutely, and we will out of nowhere be flooded with spiritualist dreams that may cause us to feel crazy and wild.

Charkas look like a hole of a camera point of convergence that when opened are overpowered with light, with essentialness with information. To snap a photograph, to record every single motivation behind reflection, the hole need simply open rapidly to get countless minute nuances.

It's the identical with the third eye, or any of the charkas most definitely. Right when the third eye opens, the mind is flooded with light, bits of information, and inspiration. This is a run of the mill reflection experience. It can happen consistently after some time, or out of nowhere. If the third eye opens wide and it's sudden, it ordinarily occurs for some time, and after that re-acclimates to another hole setting that is more open than already, yet not as far as possible open reliably.

Right, when we start to look all starry peered toward at. The heart chakra opens wide. Love spills in and gushes out. The world is prepared with likelihood and blamed for power. Furthermore, after that, our hearts settle down and get settled with the relationship. I'm assisted with recollecting the Zen saying, "First enlightenment.

By then, the dress." Some people problem of exhaustion when all the vitality fades away. This grumbling applies to the two people who have had passionate Kundalini experiences and to the people who are trapped on the surge of new love, anyway become depleted of endeavouring to keep a relationship key.

Beginning meditators report a wide scope of wonder, which aren't by and large marvel, yet rather the chief opening of the inside resources:

Visions, huge suppositions, the having a fragrance like smells that are not genuinely present, etcetera. Kundalini mixes through reflection, whether or not you put that name on it or not. Right when the mind is still, Kundalini can rise.

We each have our own outstanding explanation for the duration of regular day to day existence, and Kundalini is the transporter that transports that data to our mindfulness. Kundalini edifications are not unpredictable. However, rather, they are an affirmation of an immensely astonishing understanding at work.

KUNDALINI AS ENERGY

Kundalini is an imperativeness, which is connected to the comprehension. Twisted inside the body, it remains lazy in the resting body. This psycho-extraordinary force is mixed through various significant practices, normally appended to yoga and astral projection. Kundalini is joined to the chakras, abiding in the root chakra. Every now and again related to a snake, it will rise from the base of the spine when mixed. As the Kundalini rises, it will experience each chakra or essentialness centre, making a high-imperativeness power all through the entire body. Kundalini Yoga is the most generally perceived practice were to mix the force.

The climbing of this force can vacillate among individuals and sessions. Since the force is said to live at the base of the spine, it will rise from this bit of the body. As it blends, the yogi will begin to feel a glow around this domain as the imperativeness winds up uncoiled. As it rises, it will move upward along the spine, through the

6 diverse chakras. Right when the Kundalini experiences each essentialness centre, that chakra will end up unique and related to force. It will continue rising, taking the imperativeness of the chakras with it and leaving the body cold.

The more the Kundalini rises, the more physical reactions the yogi will have. There are consistently programmed muscle advancements or tremors, there can be a tendency of intensity or vibration, and there may in like manner, be sounds or voices. Though every kundalini stirring may not be comparably uncommon, they are consistently delineated as hazardous, inciting Out of Body Experiences, pipedreams, division, and various different genuine sensations. Like all significant and supernatural practices, Kundalini Yoga puts aside some push to expert and successful stimulating of this stunning essentialness may require some venture.

An authentic kundalini stirring will be the most uncommon experience you ever live. All of the sensations got from the convenience of your essentialness body limits will be the most remarkable you have ever observed them, and you will be amazed that you can feel such a great deal of energy, need, will, love and solidarity without an external article - for yourself, free from any other person.

Likewise, a Kundalini exciting isn't something you do. It's something that happens through you. In the state of complete loosening up and affirmation, you see your body from the start moving breathing models and position in solitude, with instant and obvious effects to the intensity of the experience, any way you know you're not the one doing it. If you can recognize this, you stay to get comfortable with a lot about the right way you should breathe in, move, and so on.

At last, as the experience ends up being progressively portrayed, the physical breath will stop. Really, you will stop unwinding. It might surrender saying that you should put forth an attempt not to drive this. You will be not able to kill yourself by compelling your breath to stop, yet you can sure as perdition cause a lot of mischiefs.

Anyway, the breath stops, and this is an entryway minute, considering the way that aside from if your mind finds a feeling of happiness and you recognize the experience, you're most likely going to hulk out and caution, being hesitant to kick the container. At the point when the breath truly, truly stops, you will see a substitute breath experiencing you - not you breathing air, yet the universe breathing you.

SIGNS OF KUNDALINI AWAKENING

Kundalini is your life power imperativeness. It's acknowledged that in the people who are unawakened, their essentialness stays circled at the base of their spine. For the people who have a breathing life into event and ended up being discerning, the imperativeness spirals upward, authorizing each chakra, and making the being change into a lit-up ace.

Various people acknowledge that a Kundalini exciting is a methodology of coming into complete nirvana, and that is substantial – partially. A Kundalini exciting is examined a lot insignificant circles considering the way that previous experiencing satisfaction, the imperativeness at first cleanses and refines, and the developments that you experience can be a terrifying, most ideal situation, and absolute anguishing much under the least ideal conditions.

A kundalini exciting can be one of the most unpleasant and perplexing occasions of your life. You can't tell toward the starting that you're truly encountering a significant cleaning process, in which you will turn out on the far edge more grounded and more sensible than whenever in ongoing memory.

Here's the best approach to realize whether you're at the same time:

1. You start a methodology of energetic retaliation. You find your cerebrum drifting through past experiences that you either miss and feel hopeless about never again having, or are lamenting for, and feel awful that you expected to involvement with any case.

2. You are emptying significant lots of stifled imperativeness hinders that have shielded you from being accessible. This suggests you'll contribute a lot of vitality altogether considering the past: what happened, and what you wish were one of a kind. This is a chance to land to an agreement with it and to release.

3. You may feel physical symptoms, for instance, arousing unpredictably hours of the night, sweating, crying, or even really feeling an unprecedented flood of essentialness going up your spine.

4. You feel a surprising need to turn out radical enhancements for a mind-blowing duration. This can consolidate everything from your eating routine to your business to the people you contribute vitality with. More than anything, you comprehend what isn't working.

5. You become mindful of how your mind has been the sole force getting you far from proximity, and from fulfilment. You begin to comprehend that your feeling of self had kept you trapped in endeavouring to "prepare for the most exceedingly horrendous," when in doubt, it was a ploy to keep you from the present moment, wherein your essentialness has it is for the most part control.

6. Awe-inspiring synchronicities begin to appear in your life. Things basically have an unpredictable strategy for working themselves out and leave you thinking: hm, that was impeccable.

7. Your sympathetic limits fortify like never before. Maybe you can think and feel accurate what another person is experiencing the moment they are experiencing it. This may overwhelm from the beginning, yet it's incredibly a sign that your third eye is opening and you're finding a good pace with your genuine nature, which is connectedness.

8. You feel a convincing drive to be outside, in nature, as much of the time as could sensibly be normal.

9. You feel a convincing drive to tidy up your life from different points of view as would be judicious: broken associations, messes in your

home, old penchants that are holding you down... everything needs to go.

10. You start to truly address immense quantities of the systems and structures that by and by exist. You begin to see things like religion and administrative issues and show in a way you never have, recognizing the root need they serve in people.

11. You experience "sporadic" combinations of feeling. Truth be told, you're overseeing old assessments you never totally tended to.

12. You feel a huge ought to be of an organization to others. You understand that as we are generally essentially one, devoting your life to the partner of others is the noblest and fulfilling thing you can do.

13. You begin to feel irate for what you were and weren't given, for all the torment you did and didn't have to adjust to. Over the long haul,

that shock breaks down into affirmation, as you believe each to be of your experience as a significant part of your experience, not an adversary to it.

14. You comprehend that life was rarely unfolding; it was basically an impression of you. What you were putting out into the world was precisely what you were getting back.

15. You feel a mysterious, private relationship with the ideal. You believe yourself to be a celestial being and see the god in one another individual alive.

16. You comprehend that you can't hold up one more moment to start living, since life is going on the present minute, and reliably has been. You begin to comprehend that you have denied yourself your bliss by holding on for it to begin.

Bit by bit directions to Awaken Your Kundalini:
7 Kundalini Awakening Techniques

There are heaps of techniques and practices that are said to help bolster your thriving or assist you with achieving singular fulfilment. This makes it extraordinary to figure out what will really work for you, and what is misdirecting or basically unhelpful. In addition, scrutinizing through personal development, composing reveals numerous new words with frustrating ramifications, so you may be allured to simply shrug and continue ahead. In any case, before you oust the probability of kundalini, see this concept could be the thought you've been keeping it together for.

Have you anytime wished you had progressively conspicuous clearness about the world and your place in it? The capacity to see and feel what you should do with your life, and the ability to fathom most of your emotions? In case the reactions to these requests are 'yes', Kundalini Awakening is the method that will get you what you need. This immediate guide will walk you through what you need to do and why.

In case you have to mix your Kundalini, you need to clear your prana (or life power) from its enthusiastic focus on contemplations about the outside world. You ought to make techniques for isolating your resources from what goes on in your physical body, as it's at precisely that point that you can find a workable pace essentialness of the Kundalini.

As you may know from care or examination works out, it will in general test to do roll out such an improvement in any occasion, for a moment, it wouldn't fret for expanded time allotments. Regardless, even one moment of achievement can begin to change the way in which you think and centre intrigue! With taking a shot at, changing the prana in the correct way can end up being normal.

The inspiring news I that a huge amount of the thing you can do to mix your Kundalini simply require turning out little enhancements your customary everyday presence. Here are seven of the most prevailing procedures.

1.   Focus on Your Breath

Anything that empowers you to revolve around your breath moreover causes you to move towards a Kundalini Awakening. This suggests if you starting at now have a standard reflection or care routine with respect to the sort referenced above, you're well on your way to deal with exploiting your Kundalini imperativeness.

In any case, don't give up on the off chance that you're just starting to comprehend frameworks like this! Taking everything into account, the least troublesome structures are much of the time the best.

For example, have a go at experiencing just five minutes focusing on significant unwinding. Take in through the nose and inhale out through the mouth, breathing from your stomach rather than your chest.

Yoga (not just Kundalini yoga) is another phenomenal development for focusing the breath. Whether or not you're an expert or an absolute beginning, tackling yoga presents at the start or day's end can be incredibly valuable. Also, just review that you don't need to put excessive proportions of vitality in these exercises to have any sort of impact!

2.   Reject Negativity

As you'll certainly realize whether you're alright with Law of Attraction and sign work, vitality is basic to making delight. In particular, you need to tackle viably expelling negativity in case you have to mix your Kundalini.

Most of us are verified in pointless instances of thinking. Nevertheless, by attempting to make another strategy for seeing the world, you bit by bit give new inclinations that stick.

Likely the best framework for rejecting cynicism is reframing. At whatever point you find yourself considering yourself or your general environment, challenge yourself to redo it in an undeniably positive way.

For example, "It's too much cold outside to go for a run today" advances toward turning out to be "I have the whole night to spend on something I acknowledge inside". Even more radically, something as "I didn't land the situation since I'm pointless" pushes toward turning out to be "I didn't land this situation considering the way that the right one is coming around the curve".

3.   Keep A Good Posture

There's a close-by an association between the physical body and the charging of the Kundalini.

In particular, it's basic to look out for your position and make changes as central.

In a case like a large number of individuals, you have a modestly idle action that incorporates expanded timeframes at a PC, and you may be slanted to slumping with round shoulders.

In like manner, stress may leave you withheld muscles, and low confidence can lead you to make your body deliberately more diminutive.

The essential concern you need to do is keep your spine straight with the objective that your back is long and tall. These not noble motivations you in your excursion to mix your Kundalini however then again is better for your whole body, reducing issues with unending misery.

If it's difficult for you to think about your position from the start, have a go at setting an hourly recommendation to fix your spine.

Following a week or something to that effect, you won't require the update any more.

4.   Access The Central Channel

You probably won't have thought about the central channel already, yet have certainty that the methods required to find a workable pace commonly direct.

•   First, guarantee you're sitting calmly, and breathe in significantly while you check to ten.

•   Next, revolve around your tailbone domain, until you can identify a fragile vibration. Presently, close your eyes and again and again serenade "Vum."

•   As you serenade, see the impression of vibration gradually working their way up to your spine. Imagine yourself skimming, light and free, radiating liberality to all your experience.

• Change your serenade, reiterating "Shum" over and over as you feel the vibrations spread all through your limbs and fill your whole body.

• Finally, picture a gigantic inflatable sitting in your pelvic and stomach locale, occupying the space there.

• Gradually let the ventilate of that inflatable, as though you're holding it by the neck and carefully recognizing everything inside.

There are progressively unpredictable exercises for finding a workable pace channel, anyway these beginnings the strategy.

You may, in like manner find entrancing could help find a workable pace channel! Self-hypnotizing can help loosen up, become focused, and mix your kundalini essentialness underneath your spine. Find internal satisfaction and manage your prosperity with this kundalini instituting stupor.

5.   Use Visualization

Recognition exercises are mind-blowing resources in every single ordinary issue, and it's in like manner key to exciting the Kundalini.

In case you look at resources on Kundalini yoga, explicitly, you'll see a tedious subject of light portrayals. One of the most notable and immense is the Divine Light Invocation, and it's definitely not hard to do, whether or not you're a student.

Start by standing up as straight as could reasonably be expected, spreading your feet until they're about shoulder-width isolated.

Next, softly close your eyes and move them upwards, so they're looking towards the focal point of the base bit of your temples. As you do this, raise your arms over your head and hold all of your muscles tight.

Repeat the going with, imagining yourself washed in splendid, white light: "Divine light makes me. Brilliant light backings me. Heavenly light verifies and envelops me. I am continually forming into marvellous light."

6.   Activate Your Interests

Like tackling your position, inciting your tendencies isn't helpful for empowering a Kundalini stimulating. It's moreover key to continuing with an energetic, well-sound way of life!

In any case, to have the alternative to exploit the Kundalini imperativeness holding up inside you, it's fundamental that you experience at any rate an hour day by day on something you truly appreciate. You may believe that its difficult to fight the social weight that says you should experience reliably on productive development, anyway sharing to your most noteworthy favourable position is useful.

Envision a situation wherein you're never again sure where your tendencies untruth. Try making a summary of 10-15 things you've for a very long time been tingling to do, without blue-pencilling yourself in any way. In any occasion, one of a kind small something can't abstain from being something you can start getting the hang of, trying or moving toward today. Moreover, in case you find an interest never again satisfies you, essentially forsake it with no-fault. Euphoric living is crucial for exciting your Kundalini.

7.   Cut Out Distractions

Finally, we, in general experience our days enveloped by potential things that can redirect us. Our thought is pulled from numerous points of view immediately, and we may feel that its hard to centre on a single thing for astoundingly critical stretches. Nevertheless, when we let our minds consistently move from thing to thing, we pack apparently in a way that denies us suitable access to the imperativeness of our Kundalini.

Remember, what is required is another partition from external things, to make space for another kind of thinking and feeling to create.

To battle interferences, it's critical to examine your living space and penchants to see what you can live without. Improve your home and your day by day plan.

Likewise, consider unplugging from the Internet every so often, or in any occasion setting up a program increase that limits your time on goals that advance postponing!

Investigating Your Awakening

While there are numerous positive signs and things that can go very right with kundalini arousing, it likewise happens to be the situation that, occasionally, it doesn't work out as you'd think. Here and there, it doesn't appear as though it's in any event, turning out by any stretch of the imagination. In those occasions, this part is here to help. We'll investigate three distinct subjects that could be influencing your procedure. To start with, we'll consider what may be keeping you down. Second, we'll take a gander at the potential perils and dangers that may be meddling with your procedure. Third lastly, we'll inspect the most widely recognized missteps individuals make in their enlivening procedure, alongside how you can expertly stay away from them. Before the finish of this part, you ought to have discovered your own foul-up, and you ought to have the option to work at adjusting it right away.

12 Things That Could Be Holding You Back

There is such a large integer of things that could be deadening you on your excursion. From enthusiastic battles to physical ones or from going excessively quick to excessively slow, there are different approaches to incidentally get in your own particular manner; however, this area will help you, in any event, open your eyes and acknowledge what you can do to help.

Physical difficulties

The straightforward reality of the situation is that occasionally our bodies aren't prepared for kundalini arousing yet. At times, it's because of an auto-invulnerable issue. Now and again, it's brought about by an absence of capacity in a specific piece of the body. Once in a while, still, it's brought about by the powerlessness to rehearse reflection because of broad everyday tension. Notwithstanding the physical difficulties that are holding you up, you are not a disappointment.

You will go to a point in your mending when you have the option to deal with kundalini arousing over everything else, except right currently probably won't be that minute, and that is alright.

Surging one's kundalini arousing can be adverse some of the time, and it's in every case best to simply take it at a pace that feels regular and non-distressing for your experience and needs.

Encountering things with an excess of force or too rapidly

Now and again, the chakras aren't that blocked, and they're moderately simple to open, purge, and adjust. For individuals that have this experience, the kundalini arousing procedure may happen a lot quicker than it would for the standard, profoundly blocked person. If so for you, you'll likely have an unimaginably serious encounter directly from the earliest starting point, and it could even turn out to be too extraordinary in light of the speed of progress. In case you're not hurrying things they're despite everything progressing strongly and speedier than foreseen, attempt to contemplate each other day. Attempt to make a stride back in your procedure and permit it to get more settled, rescaled to foresee what you can deal with. You may likewise profit colossally from having a guide or master. A few people don't do well with these sorts of connections in mending and arousing, but since you're so exceptionally touchy, an educator or coach even only a listening supporter–might be only the thing.

Diet doesn't bolster arousing

It might sound implausible to a few (and I'd be happy to wager this "a few" gathering of individuals is contained for the most part of meat-eaters), yet here and there, your eating regimen will hinder your enlivening. Saying that doesn't mean you have to feel free to remove meat or dairy or gluten or sugar. It all the more so implies that you might have the option to help your enlivening procedure on the off chance that you make a couple of slight alterations. You can begin by eating less handled nourishment and more products of the soil. In the event that that is difficult for you to do to begin, take a stab at starting by eating one less supper with meat every week. Just beginning little and perceive how you feel; perceive how your body responds.

On the off chance that a positive reaction is evoked, roll out extra improvements in understanding.

You're concentrating on an inappropriate body part

A few issues with kundalini arousing are established in the person's capacities to centre, and these issues are effectively balanced with a switch of where one's consideration goes when the individual ponders. For instance, particularly on the off chance that you centre your vitality into your head (or into your third eye) when you shut your eyes to reflect (which the vast majority do), you've discovered your concern in that spot. To prompt kundalini arousing, you have to begin by centring your vitality into your heart, gut, and gut. The kundalini needs a solid domain to ascend into, and in case you're sending such sound consideration regarding your third eye, you've skipped path past that gut space that the kundalini meets first. Consider how the kundalini will move and set up your body as needs are. Basically, during your contemplations, inhale profoundly into your stomach for some time and see what changes for you.

Your attitude overlooks the body or the other way around

In light of where kundalini arousing originated from—in the present day, with Yogi

Bhajan and his act of kundalini yoga—it bodes well that your act of enlivening can't simply be mental so as to succeed. It must be offset with physical endeavours, as you're ready to finish them. The association with yoga is significant here, for that training can do a ton to help in your kundalini's enlivening. Fundamentally, kundalini yoga particularly rinses blockages in one's chakras through the development and body-centred relaxing. In a similar vein, one can't induce full kundalini arousing through simply the act of yoga.

There must be a harmony between mind-based and body-based methodologies in your general endeavour. Else, you will proceed right now interior lopsidedness.

Poor Or Unsupportive State Of Mind

In a specific way, kundalini arousing can help straighten out mind-set and passionate lopsided characteristics, yet one needs to find a workable pace first. It may be the case that those elevated state of mind and passionate irregular characteristics are what's keeping you from any away from in your expectations of enlivening. Check your attitude!

Check your most basic dispositions! In the event that there's any way you can start to alter those mentalities and temperaments, you're certain to see some distinction in your kundalini practice in a matter of seconds. It might sound entangled, pushy, or troublesome now, yet in the event that you can by one way or another ascent over any depleting dispositions and feelings, you'll see your kundalini ascend in kind.

Overpowering inclinations for control

The facts demonstrate that perfect kundalini enlightenments occur with definitely no exertion in the interest of the individual; however, not all renewals can happen that way.

In any case, there are numerous interruptions obstructing the awesome that is fundamentally wherever nowadays. Eventually, there ought to be no sense of self-based driving, pushing, or controlling associated with one's enlivening. In any case, this entire book,, despite everything helps its peruser through methods and tips to help in their independently directed arousing, so it extremely just comes down to finding a parity. In case you're battling with the procedure, attempt to set up a superior harmony among self guidance and attempting to do a lot of too immediately, at that point see what occurs.

Past injury or PTSD is excessively solid of a blockage

In some cases, the injuries we took the stand concerning before (or that we're as of now enduring) make blockages for us that become so dug in thus pervasively spread all through the chakras that we become unfit to direct ourselves through our own enlightenment. That is not a positive or negative thing; it's essentially an unavoidable truth. In the event that you feel that this opinion concerns you, don't be put off from kundalini arousing, for there is mind-boggling and life-changing trust in you. It just implies that you may need to work through your injuries independently first. In light of what you've encountered, it might be strong to converse with somebody about that experience, regardless of whether it's a companion, accomplice, gatekeeper (on this plane or another), or advisor.

Use craftsmanship treatment or music treatment on the off chance that you'd preferably not associate with someone else, you'd preferably not impart your injury to another person, or you feel that you have nobody else to impart it to. Get that yuck out by one way or another! Attempt to be imaginative or open about it, and your kundalini will begin ascending quickly.

Reluctance to confront one's actual nature

Arousing can be a precarious procedure on occasion. It's not in every case, simply positive signs and nice sentiments and satisfaction. Some of the time, you'll be made to confront your flaws,and the undertaking will be this: change them or endure no further kundalini development.

It's a predicament, yet it unquestionably implies that a few people flounder during the time spent arousing in light of these self-based rude awakenings. Moreover, as the kundalini rises at first through the throat, third eye, and crown chakras (before it begins free-moving through all the open chakras), the individual will acknowledge increasingly more how loaded up with heavenly nature the person in question is. For a few, this mindfulness is alarming or an excessive amount to deal with. Some are essentially reluctant to grasp this potential. To off-set from this circumstance in the event that you discover you're being kept down comparatively, what you can do is to rehearse radical receptiveness and acknowledgement of yourself, godlikeness, and others.

No people group of help

In the event that you've at any point heard somebody state that kundalini arousing would take your loved ones from you, you've likely quite recently cooperated with somebody who attempted to discuss their enlivening with those nearest to the person in question, yet the network couldn't or wouldn't bolster those endeavours. This rejection of enlivening doesn't generally occur, and regardless of whether it happens to you with respect to your dear companions or family, don't let yourself get excessively down in the mouth yet! around are a couple of things you can do right now. (1) Leave kundalini arousing out of it where these individuals are included on the grounds that (2) as you proceed on your enlivening excursion, your forces of fascination will be more grounded than any time in recent memory.

With the correct mix of expectation and centre, you'll without a doubt attract to you the correct network of help right away. (3) You can likewise continue attempting with those loved ones, just with various strategies whenever. (4) You could even reject the possibility of a steady network totally and assemble one yourself with data. There are plenty of applications you can download that will help support your enlivening with strong tips and counsel, and for certain individuals, this data switch is sufficient to compensate for what individuals around them need.

No educator or guide

While a few people will act naturally guided in their renewals with no issue, others improve toward that involvement in an educator or if nothing else a tutor helping and directing their ways. In the event that you feel lost and are urgently looking for an instructor, my first proposal is to search out a yoga studio that educates kundalini yoga. Startup a discussion with the educator there and see what blooms from that point. On the other hand, you could search out kundalini chatrooms on the web, or on the off chance that you incline toward things face to face, you could go to your neighbourhood magical store and make an inquiry or two about reflection guides. You never need to battle alone. Let kundalini control your certainty to empower you to attract the individuals whose assist you'll with requiring for development.

Situations don't bolster arousing

Regardless of whether it's your home condition, your workplace, your financial condition, your common habitat, or else, the facts demonstrate that a few spaces don't line up with one's endeavouring toward arousing. At times, individuals go on and on, which can influence your stream. Now and again, individuals may giggle at you for what you're enthusiastic about. Different occasions, you may be encompassed with contaminations that keep, for instance, your pineal organ calcified without your knowing. Trust your instinct here. In the event that it feels like a dangerous spot to contemplate or do your yoga practice, attempt to discover another space.

On the off chance that it feels like your prosperity and rational soundness is undermined by being what your identity is and doing what you need to do, look for cover somewhere else for this endeavour until you're sufficiently able to battle that vibe. You don't need to compel this procedure, and you absolutely don't need to do it where you can't have a sense of security.

10 Dangers and Risks Associated with Awakening

While "threat" is a solid word to depict it, genuinely, there are a few perils related to arousing, especially as far as going for beyond what you can deal with. This segment will unequivocally list 10 dangers so you can check whether you're moving toward things such that is riskier than would normally be appropriate. On the off chance that you identify with any of these 10 focuses, you will need to change your methodology in the event that you ever would like to see genuine and enduring accomplishment with kundalini arousing.

Nonetheless, a portion of these "threats" are simply indications that may terrify you when you experience them, and the fact is simply to work through them. I'll note when this case is valid for a specific supposition.

Overburdening or overpowering the spirit

There's consistently the danger of profoundly overexerting yourself. Whenever one powers or attempts to launch kundalini arousing, this hazard is extremely present. Particularly, in case you're not in contact with your higher self or soul guides, you may have an incredibly hard time acknowledging where your chakras are blocked and how precisely to clear them. Besides, you may not understand until past the point of no return in case you're overpowering the kundalini and arousing process in general, driving your spirit to deal with more than what it's prepared for. The best strategy is to simply accept out of this world without attempting to do a lot on the double.

Doing things to an extreme and too rapidly

There's an equivalent hazard for the individuals who attempt to do excessively and too rapidly. This strategy in all likelihood causes irregularity later, as the constrained and stimulated kundalini is made to frenzy through your framework's vibration and to some degree overlook blockages in the chakras it goes through. This activity, in general, harms one's kundalini and makes expansion conditions of sickness in one's chakras, so please pay attention to me here.

Be mindful so as not to do an excess of too rapidly so you won't have considerably more stuff to work through later on when you're prepared to attempt once more.

Your body can't stay aware of the brain

Here and there, you won't generally realize you're doing excessively and too rapidly on the grounds that it's everything occurring within. In these cases, all things considered, your body can't stay aware of the speed that your brain can deal with. Like the point simply over, this issue can mean future chakra uneven characters and harms to your emanation and kundalini, so the best activity accordingly is to ensure that your training applies a mix of body-based and mind-based practices.

Pondering and reciting is a certain something; however, it can't be only this articulation without yoga and in any event, running or cycling, as well. Adjust your body to your brain, and you won't have this issue.

Absence of groundedness because of profound "highs."

As you work through and into the profundities of your enlivening, you may get yourself profoundly "high" now and again, and you will be substantially less grounded in your earthen body at whatever point this happens. This "risk" is increasingly similar to a manifestation, as referenced in the acquaintance passage with this segment. The vast majority will encounter this unfoundedness through the energy of the kundalini arousing. Your higher chakras will be opened wide, and you will stand the opportunity to be diverted by what you can see now. At whatever point you feel like this–marvellous, diverted, floaty, nearly cloud-like–begin breathing profoundly. Make one hand into a clench hand at your navel and envision that you can drop a line from this spot in your body straight down into the earth. As this string drops and associates with nature, feel grounded and avowed with your human body. This representation should straightforwardness such "high" indications at whatever point they come up.

Jerkiness and muscle fits

Likewise, with the point straightforwardly above, jerkiness and muscle fits are side effects of kundalini arousing that many (if not all) will involvement with their procedures. It just becomes coded as a "hazard" or "threat" on the grounds that the individual probably won't imagine that these activities are associated with their enlivening and get terrified for their own prosperity. If at any time you do have these fits or automatic rascals, inhale profoundly and attempt to feel quiet. These are regular "developing torments" related to arousing, and they will pass. In the long run, you won't have them at all any longer, yet for the present, inhale profoundly and acknowledge them. They're a decent sign, in all honesty.

Getting yourself alone in the "dull night of the spirit."

Another manifestation of enlivening is the experience of the "dim night of the spirit."

This timeframe will happen for any engaged with kundalini arousing, and it's not really an enjoyable time, which is the reason it's coded as a "threat" or "hazard." Essentially, the "dull night of the spirit" is the point at which you have an inclination that you've hit you're least low. It's the minute after you face all the defects in yourself and acknowledge you can just move upwards, which is an overwhelming obligation. You may lose somebody near you, similar to a guide, companion, or adored one. You may wind up feeling aimless or addressing all that you thought you knew was valid and genuine and great. In the event that you wind up feeling these things, you haven't fizzled at arousing yourself; realize that to the profundities of your centre. You have not fizzled; you're spot on the track. For the individuals who know somebody genuinely delicate who's attempting kundalini arousing, keep close tabs on that individual. The genuinely delicate among us stand incredible hazard while experiencing these periods alone. On the off chance that they're excessively aimless and down and out, it can mean their lives; however, we can generally secure against that. We are more grounded as a network together, and every one of us will endure this dull night with that sponsorship quality.

Inconvenience acclimating to a new perspective

At the point when you go into arousing, you may not understand every one of that needs to change. Your association with mainstream society, music, news, media, prescription, and more will completely and without a doubt, change. A manifestation of these modifications that occasionally acts like a "hazard" or "threat" is that individuals can experience difficulty grappling with the new perspective. In the event that you identify with this message, make an effort not to battle what you're realizing. Practice open and radical acknowledgement and recollect that you would not be indicated these things on the off chance that it wasn't essential for your spirit and your kundalini arousing. Trust known to man and accept significantly that the world is as yet excellent without what you thought you knew.

Kundalini disorder looks like steady nerves and tension with so-called "dreams of greatness". Individuals with the disorder live for the most part in a difficult situation identifying with the physical earth plane. These individuals are stuck in a period of enlivening, and that stuck-ness could have been brought about by compelling the procedure, speeding it up, or working through it for polluted aim.

To keep away from the disorder for yourself, accept incredibly with your enlivening and don't get too worried when circumstances become difficult. Accept with your heart that you will discover parity and simplicity again. You will make it to the opposite side of enlivening, and afterward, with that conviction planted somewhere down in your heart, you're certain not to stall out.

CHAPTER TWO

ADVANTAGES OFAWAKENED KUNDALINI

It shows up we are clueless concerning data about kundalini, sadly, various spiritualist and clairvoyants are deluding people with respect to this subject. So the request does come up, what are the kundalini stirring advantages? It's not something we can boast to friends and family or in online systems. Truth remains kundalini requires various significant lots of significant work, both mental and physical.

In all cases, kundalini is slow from birth. Having said that after the kundalini released or blended, the essentialness shoots up your spine, causing various mental changes inside you. This is in light of the fact that the chakras have opened during the kundalini stimulating. Exactly when a complete kundalini exciting occurs, all of the seven chakras or imperativeness centres in your body are open, for the most part, it's ridiculous.

Various people commit for as far back as they can recall to having their kundalini mix by practising examination and significant work, they may experience the kundalini exciting from a half year to even decades, yet arranged yogis will all in all have revived outcomes. One of the strategies to mix your kundalini is through shaktipat, and the technique incorporates being accessible to essentialness with hard and fast surrender and wants.

Note: Please don't force yourself into a kundalini stirring, You may achieve more mischief than extraordinary.

If you are one who is open to the comprehensive imperativeness, the kundalini stirring system will be smoother for you rather than be an unconstrained thing. So what are the kundalini stirring advantages? Various who have encountered this methodology report the going with preferences of kundalini exciting.

In addition, when blended, the lazy essentialness shoots up the spine, causing various critical changes. Perhaps the most noteworthy of these is opening of the chakras, the essentialness centres that direct our vivacious body.

Every one of the seven must be open altogether for the Kundalini to rise. There are various people who have dedicated for as far back as they can recollect to exciting their Kundalini by practising consideration and supernatural work. It really takes that much effort. If you are one who is responsive to the comprehensive imperativeness, the Kundalini exciting system will be smoother for you rather than be an unconstrained thing. So what are the Kundalini stirring advantages?

1.   Feeling increasingly settled and euphoria

2.   Increase in IQ level

3.   The much better sentiment of sound, concealing and sight

4.   A notion of sterilization

5.   Psychic limits are improved

6.   More compassion and empathy

7.   Slowed down developing and augmentation in ingenuity

8.   Blissful vibration of imperativeness saw inside the ears as sound (om)

9.   You become progressively alluring and can attract conditions or people into your reality with your thoughts

10.   Increased significant affiliation

11.   Become truly strong and really relentless

12.   Feeling thoughtfulness regarding cleaning

Kundalini Awakening benefits through heading

Exactly when the Kundalini is mixed, it is essentially a conclusive device improvement, allowing long stretch positive change. The possibility of Kundalini is that it can't be held down when the courses are open; there is no genuine method to stop it. That is the explanation it's an exceptional idea to find heading through lit-up ean ducator.

Kundalini exciting can be overwhelming and frightening; similarly, it's essential and amazingly earth-shattering. As the essentialness climbs your spine, like a circled snake, the experience can be euphoric, ,or it will, in general, be incredibly disturbing, phenomenal and feel loathsome. One thing we can make sure about is where the Kundalini is mixed, the presence we understand will never be comparable again. One of the Kundalini stimulating advantages every now and again fathomed is where the essentialness climbs your spine, your unaware contemplations can be displayed as mindful thoughts. Nothing will be secured, whether or not you have to oversee it or not. It will be out there. That is one motivation behind why Kundalini stimulating shouldn't be done alone, without an instructor who can control you through this over the top enthusiastic technique.

CHAPTER THREE
PRANA

Prana is a Sanskrit word that unravels as "basic life power." Understanding what prana is and how it capacities takes after being given a key that can open new,, improved degrees of prosperity and thriving—on the overall.

Prana is the broad sea of essentialness that instilsand vitalizes all issue. This sea of imperativeness consolidates into sub-atomic particles and particles, which become the basic structure squares of all issue demonstrating the physical world. Thusly, every molecule, iota, and cell is a development of prana, correspondingly as waves are growthof the sea that lies underneath them.

The five key assets of our inclination—the mind, breath (prana), talk, hearing, and sight—were battling about which was the most huge. To decide the inquiry they picked that each would leave the body along these lines to see whose nonappearance was missed most. The first talk left, yet the body continued flourishing anyway it hushed up. Next,, the eye left, yet the body flourished anyway outwardly impeded. By then the ear left, yet the body thrived anyway almost deaf. Finally,, ,the mind left, yet still,, the body lived on, anyway it was by and by unmindful. In any case, the moment the prana started to leave, the body began to fail miserably. Various assets were rapidly losing their life-power, so they all dashed to prana, yielded its incredibleness, and begged it to remain.

This is an old Vedic story, possibly different interpretations of which are found in various Upanishads. The conflict, in any case, addresses the normal human condition where our assets are not fused, anyway rival each other for control of our thought. When prana leaves, it ends up being sure that prana offers essentialness to all of our assets, without which none of them can work. Thusly the exercise of this story is that to control these assets, one must control the prana.

To accomplish positive changes in body and mind, we ought to understand the imperativeness through which they work. This force is called prana in Sanskrit, meaning "basic essentialness," now and again deciphered as "breath" or "principal power," anyway it is truly something more. The different structures through which prana conveys are just every now and then assessed all around in Western composition on yoga, and in this manner, the investigation of prana, which is colossal and huge, is now and again appreciated.

Prana has various degrees of criticalness, from the physical breath to the imperativeness of mindfulness itself. Prana isn't only the fundamental life-oblige; it is the principal imaginative force. It is the expert sort of all essentialness working at every level of our being. In actuality, the entire universe is an indication of prana. Without a doubt, even kundalini shakti, the snake control or internal imperativeness which changes our insight, makes from mixed prana.

On an immense level, there are two pieces of prana. The first is unmanifest, the essentialness of unadulterated awareness, which transcends all creation. The second, or show prana, is basically the intensity of creation. The Purusha, or higher Self, can be said to be unmanifest prana, the essentialness of perception itself, called devatma shakti or chiti shakti. From the unmanifest prana of unadulterated care comes the show prana of creation, through which the entire universe shows up.

Nature itself is made out of three gunas, or attributes: sattva, or understanding, which offers rise to the cerebrum; rajas, or advancement, which offers climb to prana; and tamas, or inaction, which offers rise to the physical body. Nature is a working, or rajasic, imperativeness. Responding to the draw of the higher Self, or unadulterated discernment, this essentialness advances toward turning out to be sattvic. By the idleness of deadness, this equal essentialness advances toward turning out to be tamasic.

Near with our physical nearness, prana or significant imperativeness is a modification of the air part, getting essentially from the oxygen we unwind. On a subtle level, the air part identifies with the sentiment of touch; through touch, we feel stimulated and can transmit our life-capacity to others.

Prana is furthermore the force that streams in each living structure and performs urgent limits. Paramhansa Yogananda called this piece of prana "life-power." He further explained that life-power has a trademark understanding engaging it to do the life-proceeding with techniques.

To offer clarity to this image, he even conceived the articulation "lifetrons." We have a subtle or astral body made up of prana that underlies the physical body. Oriental recovering strategies, for instance, Ayurveda and needle treatment, work to fit and brace the movement of life-power, calling it contrastingly prana, chi, or ki. Right when the life-power streams properly, the result will be a trademark state of prosperity and essentialness.

Prana is furthermore used to insinuate the breath. Exactly when we take a physical breath, there is a relating improvement of prana in the simple or astral spine. Prana streams up in the unnoticeable spine identified with the internal breath, and down with the exhalation.

This association among breath and the movement of prana is essential to a critical number of the techniques of thought. By controlling the breath, which is successfully felt, we can affect the movement of prana, which is extensively progressively subtle and difficult to feel.

The Koshas

The individual involves five koshas or "sheaths":

1. Annamaya kosha ("sheath made of sustenance"). This is the physical body, made out of the five parts we ingest (earth, water, air, fire, ether).

2. Pranamaya kosha ("sheath made of breath"). This is the crucial body, made out of five pieces of prana called vayus.

3. Manomaya kosha ("sheath of impressions"). This is the outer, or lower level, of mind, stacked up with the five sorts of material impressions.

4. Vijnanamaya kosha ("sheath of musings"). This is information itself, facilitated mental activity.

5. Anandamaya kosha ("sheath of experiences"). This is the more significant character, containing the memory, subliminal character, and superconscious mind.

The pranamaya kosha is anastounding circle energyThis sheath intervenes between the physical body on one side and the three sheaths of the mind (outside character, information, and inward character) on the other. It similarly mediates between the five gross parts and the five unmistakable impressions.

The best English articulation for the pranamaya kosha is likely "basic sheath" or "critical body," to get a term from Sri Aurobindo's Integral Yoga. The pranamaya kosha, which is related to the five motor organs (excretory, urino-genital, feet, hands, and vocal organ), contains our tendencies for continuance, multiplication, advancement, and self-enunciation. It outfits us with fervor and motivation for all that we do.

Pranayama (prana = imperativeness + yama = control) is a sort of examination strategy that incorporates various techniques for controlling the breathing, with the goal being to raise one's prana (moreover called Kundalini for this circumstance) up the significant spine to the extraordinary eye or sixth chakra, which conveys one to light. Kriya Yoga is one such system, made most likely comprehended by Paramhamsa Yogananda in Autobiography of a Yogi.

How Pranayama Works

On either side of the spine there is a red hot nerve channel, or nadi : ida on the left and pingala on the right.

The prana or imperativeness adventures upward through the ida nadi. With this upward improvement, the breath is therefore brought into the lungs. In like manner, the mind is pulled in outward to the universe of the resources.

The prana or essentialness adventures upward through the ida nadi. With this upward advancement, thc breath is therefore brought into the lungs. As needs be, the mind is pulled in outward to the universe of the resources.

The essentialness by then journeys downwards through the pingala nadi. Exactly when the imperativeness is going down, it is called apana rather than prana. This slipping advancement is joined by physical exhalation, and implies a rejection of external conditions.

One sign of this cycle is the relationship of internal breath with enthusiasm and delight, and exhalation with demolition and melancholy. Euphoria and wretchedness ought to reliably seek after one another when the explanation behind each is external conditions, which are ceaselessly advancing.

In any case, through pranayama systems an individual can rather redirect the imperativeness through the significant spine in the ida and pingala, called the sushumna. Exactly when the level of essentialness in the sushumna lands at the most noteworthy purpose of the spine and goes into the significant eye, or sixth chakra, one winds up lit up.

Most by far of us are directed by the central body and its significant arranged urges, which are fundamental with the objective for us to remain alive. The fundamental body is simply the home of the subliminal picture, which harbors our various sentiments of fear, needs, and associations. An enormous part of us devour our time on earth searching for satisfaction through this kosha as material pleasure and acquiring material articles.

People with a strong basic body can interest their character on the world and often become prominent for the duration of regular day to day existence. Those with a weak principal body don't have the essentialness to accomplish a great deal, and ordinarily remain in subordinate positions. Generally people with strong yet self assimilated fundamental natures run the world. Nonetheless, this nature can be maybe the best obstacle on the significant path since it makes it difficult for the person to offer up to any higher force or to examine their own hankering based main thrusts.

This makes a couple of individuals think significant life anticipates that us should smother our prana, yet a strong pranamaya kosha is one of a kind comparable to prideful or need organized vitality. It gets its quality not from singular force anyway from our offer up to the imperativeness of the amazing. Without a strong spiritualized pranamaya kosha, we miss the mark on the imperativeness to do our practices in an unprecedented and proceeded with way.

In Hindu old stories this higher prana is symbolized by the monkey god Hanuman, offspring of the breeze, whose story is told in the outdated Indian excellent the Ramayana. Hanuman offered up to the sublime as the heavenly appearances Rama and his significant other, Sita, and he thusly got the ability to advance toward turning out to be as enormous or as meager as he wished, to vanquish all foes and obstructions, and to accomplish the awesome. Such a significantly organized essential nature has imperativeness, intrigue, and enthusiasm, nearby the ability to control the resources and vital urges—all subordinate to a higher will and objective.

The Five Pranas in Yoga

The pranamaya kosha is made out of the five pranas, similarly called vayus or "forces of the air." These five pranas are arranged by improvement and bearing. This is a critical point in Ayurvedic medicate similarly as in yogic practices.

Prana Vayu

•   Prana vayu really connotes "forward-moving air," since it moves inside and regulates a wide scope of social affair into the body, from eating, drinking, and taking in, to the get-together of unmistakable impressions and mental experiences. It is propulsive in nature, getting things going and guiding them, and it gives the essential essentialness that drives us for the duration of regular day to day existence.

Apana Vayu

• Apana vayu, "the air that moves away," moves slipping and outward, regulating a wide range of end and engendering (which furthermore has a plunging improvement). It oversees the finish of stool and pee, the removing of semen, menstrual fluid, and the undeveloped organism, and the finish of carbon dioxide through the breath. On a progressively significant level, it controls the finish of negative material, energetic, and mental experiences. It is the reason of our safe limit.

Udana Vayu

• Udana vayu, "the upward-moving air," goes up and accomplishes emotional or transformative advancements of the life-imperativeness. It oversees the advancement of the body and the ability to stay, similarly as talk, effort, energy, and will. It is our standard positive essentialness, helping us to develop our different sheaths and to create in insight.

Samana Vayu

• Samana vayu, "modifying air," moves from the periphery to the center, through a beating and seeing action. It helps retention on all levels, working in the gastrointestinal tract to process sustenance, in the lungs to process air or acclimatize oxygen, and in the mind to process understanding—material, enthusiastic, and mental.

Vyana Vayu

• Vyana vayu, "outward-moving air," moves from the center to the periphery, regulating dispersal on all levels. It moves sustenance, water, and oxygen all through the body, and keeps our sentiments and thoughts hovering in the cerebrum, giving vitality and giving quality.

The five pranas can moreover be found similar to their body territory. Prana vayu supervises the improvement of essentialness beginning from the head to the navel, which is the pranic focal point of the physical body. Apana vayu regulates the improvement of imperativeness beginning from the navel to the root chakra at the base of the spine. Samana vayu administers the improvement of imperativeness from the entire body back to the navel. Vyana vayu controls the improvement of essentialness out from the navel all through the entire body.

Udana vayu directs the improvement of essentialness from the navel up to the head

Basically, prana vayu regulates the confirmation of substances, samana manages their handling, and vyana administers the spread of enhancements. Udana manages the appearance of positive essentialness, and apana directs the finish of waste materials. This is a ton of like the working of a capable machine. Prana secures the fuel, samana changes over this fuel to imperativeness, and vyana courses the essentialness to various worksites.

Apana disposes of the waste things conveyed by the change technique. Udana manages the essentialness thusly made, engaging the machine to work reasonably.

The best approach to prosperity is to keep our pranas working in congruity. Exactly when one prana ends up imbalanced, the others will as a rule lose their equalization as well, considering the way that they are out and out associated.

Generally prana and udana balance apana, as the forces of strengthening balance those of removal. Basically vyana and samana arrange with each other in regards to advancement and tightening.

How Prana Creates the Physical Body

Without prana the physical body is near a bit of earth. Prana shapes this thick mass into various members and organs by making distinctive straightforward nerve channels, or nadis, through which it can work and invigorate net issue, forming it into various tissues and organs.

Prana vayu makes the openings and redirects in the head and psyche down to the heart. There are seven openings in the head: the two eyes, two ears, two nostrils, and a mouth. Udana vayu helps prana in making the openings in the upper bit of the body, particularly the mouth and vocal organs, considering the way that the mouth is the rule opening for the head just as for the entire body. Without a doubt, the physical body is, one may state, a development of the mouth, which is essentially the essential organ of eating and explanation.

Apana vayu makes the openings in the lower some bit of the body, those of the urino-genital and excretory systems. Samana vayu makes the openings in the highlight of the body, those of the stomach related structure, centred in the navel. It opens the channels of the absorption tracts and organs, for instance, the liver and pancreas. Vyana vayu shapes the directs taking off to the edge of the body, the arms and legs. It outlines the veins and supply courses and moreover the muscles, tendons, joints, and bones.

The navel is the essential pranic network for the physical body, or annamaya kosha ("body made of sustenance"), which is told by the stomach related structure. Net prana is taken in as sustenance through the stomach related strategy, centred in the little stomach related tract, and is held in the heavier tissues, generally muscle. Anyway, prana has diverse concentrates as well, in perspective on its ability on subtler levels.

The endeavour the essential imperativeness network for the pranamaya kosha. The straightforward prana taken in by breathing is passed on by the blood on account of the action of the heart. The head is the guideline essentialness network for manomaya kosha, or the mental sheath, which is animated by material acknowledgement, directed by the eyes and ears.

Breathing is an essential sort of pranic development in the body. Prana vayu directs internal breath; samana controls ingestion of oxygen, which happens chiefly during upkeep of the breath; and vyana manages its dispersal. Apana rules exhalation, particularly concerning the appearance of carbon dioxide. Udana controls exhalation by releasing positive essentialness through the breath, for example, in talk or song.

Prana and the Mind

Mental imperativeness is gotten from sustenance, breath, and the impressions we take in from the outside world. Prana manages the affirmation of material impressions, samana supervises their mental handling, and vyana directs mental spread. Apana rules the removal of harmful musings and negative emotions. Udana gives positive mental imperativeness, quality, and energy.

On a psychological level, prana supervises our receptivity to positive wellsprings of sustenance, feeling, and learning through the mind and resources. Exactly when agitated it causes grievous needs and insatiable desires, and we become confounded, deluded, and all-around out of evening out.

Apana manages our ability to get rid of negative thoughts and sentiments. Right when unhinged it causes gloom, and we get plugged up with the undigested experience that over-burdens us for the duration of regular day to day existence, making us horrible, covered, and frail.

Samana gives us sustenance, fulfilment, and a reasonable character. Exactly when upset, it understands association and greed. We stick to things and become contracted, stale, and possessive in our direction.

Vyana gives free improvement and self-sufficiency of mind. Exactly when agitated it can cause separation, scorn, and separation. We become inadequate to get together with others or to remain related with what we are doing.

Udana gives us joy and energy and mixes our higher significant and creative potential outcomes. Exactly when upset it can cause pride and pretentiousness, and we become ungrounded, endeavoring to go unreasonably high and putting some separation between our establishments.

Significant Aspects of the Pranas

The pranas have various unprecedented limits in yogic practices. On an extraordinary level, samana directs the space inside the heart wherein the authentic Self withstands as a fire with seven bursts. Samana deals with our inside fire, which must expend impartially. Without the agreement and evening out samana makes, we can't return significantly of our being or concentrate our cerebrum.

Vyana regulates the improvement of prana through the nadis, keeping them open, clear, clean, and even in their working. Apana shields us from negative astral effects and whimsical experiences. Prana vayu gives us the most ideal want basic for significant improvement.

Udana directs our advancement in perception and passes on the mind into the states of envisioning and significant rest, and into the after-death spaces. Udana moreover directs advancement up the sushumna. Since the mind moves with udana vayu, it is regularly the most noteworthy prana for significant improvement.

As we practice yoga, the unpretentious pieces of these pranas begin to mix, which may cause distinctive exceptional advancements of imperativeness in body and cerebrum, including diverse unconstrained improvements called kriyas. We may feel new extents of essentialness (unassuming vyana); unprecedented congruity (subtle samana); a sentiment of delicacy, as if we are suspending (unnoticeable udana); significant groundedness and unfaltering quality (unpretentious apana); or simply expanded vitality and affectability (inconspicuous prana).

Working with Prana

Authentic sustenance increases prana on a physical level. Suitable end moreover has any kind of effect. In Ayurvedic thought, the prana from sustenance is put resources into the inside organ, particularly in the upper 66% of this organ. Henceforth apana is the most critical prana for physical prosperity.

The Vedas express that people eat sustenance with apana, while the heavenly creatures eat sustenance with prana. The people are the physical tissues, proceeded by right sustenance. The immortals are the resources that take in sustenance by methods for prana itself as material impressions. To fortify prana, rehearses, for instance, customs and recognitions are huge, similarly as substantial medications including concealing, sounds, or scents, and contact with nature.

The guideline way to deal with work with prana is through pranayama, particularly as yogic breathing exercises. Yoga underlines the refinement of both body and mind as an approach to Self-affirmation, and in this way, it highlights a veggie darling eating regimen rich in prana—that is, sustenances overflowing with the life-influence—and a cerebrum built up in moral characteristics, for instance, trustworthiness and tranquillity, and in extraordinary educates. An unclean, deadly, or upset body and mind can't comprehend the higher Self. The best approach to cleaning body and mind is prana, which associations the two. The guideline system is the refinement of the nadis through which prana streams.

While all yogic breathing exercises are helpful in such a way, the most noteworthy is nadi shodhana (trade nostril breathing), which empowers equality to right and left prana streams. According to the yogic structure, the body and all of its channels have a benefit or left amazing quality. The right side is sun situated in nature. It helps in such activities as handling, work, and center, and is pittic, or singing, in constitution. The left, or the lunar, nadi is kaphic, or water predominant. It helps in such activities as rest, rest, and loosening up.

Conventional trade nostril breathing is the most noteworthy procedure for keeping our pranas or energies in leveling, yet there is another system—joining prana and apana.

Apana vayu, which is agreed with the intensity of gravity, when in doubt moves diving, occurring in illness and going just as in the plunging improvement of mindfulness. Prana vayu, of course, will by and large dissipate upward through the cerebrum and resources, and is our pathway to the energies above. Yogic practices require bringing apana up and chopping prana down so the two can consolidate; this helps balance all the pranas. In doing accordingly, the internal fire or kundalini ends up enkindled in the zone of the navel. Mula bandha (the root lock) is a critical practice in such way.

Mantra and Meditation

The pranas in the mind can be overseen honestly. There are pranayama frameworks that work with the mind and resources, and are not just obliged to the breath. Concealing and sound (music) are noteworthy ways to deal with organize imperativeness in the mind, anyway the best strategy is mantra, particularly single syllable, or bija, mantras like Om, which make vibrations that can help direct positive essentialness into the subliminal. Reflection itself, making space in the mind, serves to make more prana, and when the cerebrum is brought into a calm and open condition, like a locale of sky, another imperativeness shows up which can understand unbelievable change.

All of the methods for yoga rely upon controlling prana. Bhakti yoga, or the yoga of commitment, accomplishes pranic change by going along with us with the ideal prana. Karma yoga, or organization, relies upon course of action with the magnificent will, which in like manner gives us more prana, not only to act clearly, anyway for interior improvement.

Old style yoga, or raja yoga, relies upon the control of mental activities (chitta vrittis). The vibration of the mind (chitta spanda) seeks after the vibration of (prana spanda), and right now helps control the cerebrum. It furthermore helps control the resources (pratyahara), considering the way that it pulls back our care interior from the resources. Hatha yoga itself is mainly stressed over prana; yoga positions occur as a surge of pranic improvement, and various mind boggling yogis learned yoga positions not through mechanical practice, yet through the force of their blended prana.

Jnana yoga, or the yoga of learning, requires a strong will and center. Right now prana of solicitation must be made, which implies we ought to ask into our real nature, not just normally anyway in most of our step by step works out; without well-made udana vayu we will come up short.

Without a doubt, as the Vedas state, we are through and through affected by prana. Prana is the sun that gives life and light to everyone and stands inside the heart as the Self taking everything into account. The prana in us gives us life and empowers us to act. We should make sense of how to be accessible to and welcome this progressively significant force and hope to present to it even more totally into our life and exercises. This is maybe the best riddle of yoga.

Getting Energy and the Pranic Body

In our physical body, blood travels through veins, vessels, and hallways. In our essentialness body, prana courses through imperativeness pathways called nadis (nadi deciphers as stream).

Prana rides on the breath, so when we take in, we take in prana. Exactly when we broaden the breath and improve its tendency, we are developing and improving the idea of this central life power inside and around us. This is really what yoga breathing techniques, or pranayama, are proposed to do.

A noteworthy piece of the pranic body are the chakras, or imperativeness centers.

In yoga, we base on the seven huge chakras that exist along the line of the spine, each one related with unequivocal organs and organs of the physical body, similarly as regions of our mind that effect our character.

It is acknowledged by various that prosperity and success comes when there is a reasonable imperativeness travel through all of the seven critical chakras.

On the flipside, when prana is shielded from gushing ordinarily, either finding a good pace or overactive at a certain point, it can make disharmony on both a physical and energetic level.

In what capacity Might We Help Prana Flow Freely?

By practicing Yoga, clearly!

Yoga positions, particularly the customary or old style asanas, start express chakras. For example, Bridge Pose and Shoulder Stand work the essentialness at the throat chakra, which can affect how we talk with others.

On a physical level, the throat chakra identifies with the thyroid and parathyroid organs, and can thusly have a supporting and altering sway on our processing.

We should not disregard pranayama, the yoga breathing systems which are expressly expected to develop prana. The word yama expects to control, so when we develop and control the breath, we can intentionally broaden and pass on the basic life power inside our system.

While you don't generally need to totally get a handle on this piece of yoga to get the points of interest, practicing with energetic affectability can add another estimation to your preparation, and perhaps assist you with acknowledging progressively balanced degrees of prosperity and success.

How to understand prana?

1. Increase prana. You need more prana regardless.

2.   Conserve prana. You have to benefit and put aside money.

3.   Channel prana. You have to spend it splendidly. Use it, yet channel it.

4.   Balance prana. A lot of issue begins from ponderousness. Imperativeness is wild a great deal of this, an extreme measure of that.

5.   Purify prana. It takes after you change your 5 dollar notes to 100 dollar notes. You have to make the essentialness end up being even more predominant. Since when it ends up being progressively unadulterated it ends up being even more predominant.

Grasp why we are exhausted

•   Sometimes we think " I'm exhausted so I rest". In any case, reflection around then is better.

- You do the asanas so you can sit to reflect. At last if you will have the alternative to control the mind, you tune to the otherworldly self.

- When you are depleted, you contemplate the physical body, anyway you are not understanding that your tiredness is also starting from mental tiredness and significant tiredness.

- When you are depleted you contemplate the physical body and state " I should go get some sustenance". That infers you imply back again and again to the physical body.

- But you also have mental tiredness, mental energetic tiredness. Exactly when you are depleted maybe you have the mental tiredness since you have some negative emotions that are eating you up inside.

- You likely won't think about that. Like you dislike something or you loathe something and your keenness go off base reasoning all kind of things that are absolutely misguided.

- On top of that, the character is there, hindering the stream, so the imperativeness of unadulterated perception isn't there, and you are blocking yourself from that movement of essentialness.

The Prana Pulse

- We need to make sense of how to feel the beat of our prana reliably and when we feel that our prana is lacking with respect to, you have the choice to go to the most raised wellspring of prana, the significant prana . This absolute best kind of prana that will supply prana to the different levels.

• Any proportion of physical development won't supply the powerful prana and loosening up that you need. In any case, in case you can yield the significant prana, this will give every one of you the imperativeness to light up the entirety of your mental, excited blockages, all your deadness in your thinking, separate the mental self portrait and offer prosperity to the body.

• But if you tune just to the physical level and interpret everything truly, centering for as far back as you can recollect and mindfulness around the physical body, you are off base. Around then you starve your mental body and extraordinary body. You don't consider supernatural explanation. You put the significant behind the physical.

• So that isn't an outstandingly insightful strategy for using the Universal imperativeness open to you for your success. Remember, our flourishing is physical, mental, and energetic.

Extending prana

•   You increase prana by a wary choice of lifestyle. Lifestyle ought to be balanced and solid. Think about the manner in which that the essentialness of Nature starts from the imperativeness of the 5 key parts of Nature: Earth, water, fire, air, ether.

•   Just how you are living in nature, you are getting prana. In case you live dishonestly, you are cutting off yourself from the standard movement of prana. You live in strong, glass, and steel, neon light, no prana air. You go to shopping center, spot of business, mix with various people of no understanding, without powerful contemplations. Everyone is engaged, and voracious. You endeavor to make money to be somebody. You leave structures and step in the vehicle and drive on interstate, most of your step by step practices are fake.

Along these lines of life increases vata, and the fake ness in the mind. You land at fake home, eat counterfeit sustenance, microwave. You surf the Internet and have counterfeit associations. Would you have the option to imagine... ..

• You need to continue the physical body with nature, sit on earth, see trees, grasp a tree, look at animals. Marvel about sprout, grass. This gives you prana. Endeavor to screen, don't spend. You need to choose a smart choice of lifestyle which will give you vitality and aliveness. A portion of the time, you need to choose remarkable choices to recoup your own fulfillment.

Sparing prana

• When you are incapacitated, you lie there and you can't talk, think, or move, considering the way that your prana is absolutely down.

Imagine everything takes prana. For the duration of the day you are dynamic you are moving close. You are thinking. You experience so much prana. How might you stimulate? You can't spend more than you make.

• Daily, you have to register in your mind energetic how might you spend imperativeness. Am I achieving things today to empower? Reliably, you address with troubles and you need to proportion imperativeness spent on trivial things so you will have essentialness to address with your challenges.

• When you contribute time at the ashram, you are in conviction contributing your imperativeness to get the significant essentialness, the insight. If you get this supernatural imperativeness, you will waste less your essentialness.

• For model, in case you have a mental issue, when you have significant imperativeness, you will say "this is peanuts, this is straightforward" . All around, you need perspective of your life and what your personality is. If not, you get enraged of each apparently irrelevant detail. We spend essentialness going round, round, round.

- Sometimes you are exhausted, you would state " I'm going to eat,and visit and not go to satsang" . This infers you are not contributing cautiously your imperativeness. Be mindful so as not to waste your essentialness on things that are excess.
- That's the explanation in yoga hypothesis the savvy teacher says: isolate, independent! ... Don't pressure, don't pressure. So you can find a good pace of the issue. A comparable issue will be there, yet you can see reality with regards to it.

Coordinating prana

• Channeling imperativeness implies make your life accommodating. Use your imperativeness for generous explanation, by then you will procure significant essentialness. If you spend imperativeness for self absorbed explanation, it causes you to feel strong, yet you pay in another way, stress, defense, amassing, prideful want. It squares you so you pay the expense. It' s for no situation supported, in spite of all the difficulty in case you consider suitably.

• If you use essentialness conciliatorily, assume in organization, you get the significant imperativeness. You use your physical, mental imperativeness, yet you get thusly significant essentialness. That is known as the rule of karma yoga. It's a mindful exchange of imperativeness. It ends up significant essentialness. That powerful essentialness is mind boggling and can unwind a huge amount of blockages from already.

Modifying prana

- How you can be imbalanced? Lets state you do an exorbitant measure of physical work, you won't have enough essentialness for finding and won't have the choice to do mental work or even have feeling.

- Some others are feeling continually, they are energetic to the point that they have no essentialness for theory. They basically feel, feel, and feel. Others are thinking, thinking, and after that they have no imperativeness for sentiments. So you ought to change everything.

- It is said if you are unreasonably energetic, you would should be progressively ordinary, and think a bit. In the inverse, if an individual is unnecessarily dry, by then they need to develop their capacity of tendency. So whatever you do at the ashram you are altering yourself. Serenade a piece, think a piece, tune to the significant, and screen your physical essentialness. If you would prefer not to discuss, that is really when you need to recount to recharge your energetic imperativeness that is down and dry around at that point.

• This will build up that respectful essentialness that floods you and modify you and cause you to feel fortified. By then now and again you would incline toward not to think. Around then you ought to be caution and think. So you practice your academic essentialness.

• Sometimes you have to examine 5 hours out of each day. In the ashram you have to do physical work, in light of the fact that a huge part of us are unreasonably mental. You have to go hack wood, pass on water, tunnel channel, clean lake. This sort of physical work is similarly valuable for people with a ton of physical essentialness as it would spend that plenitude of physical imperativeness out and balance you. Else you become out of sort.

A couple of individuals are so absorbed at looking neighbor for instance they are self-held, continually worried over others' assessment of them. This glad essentialness eats up them. We must have enough of care, yet if you are eaten up by it, around then you become cut off from your higher explanation.

Wash down prana

•   This is the most interesting topic. How might you cleanse your imperativeness? You disinfect through practicing supernatural practices, by intentionally going toward a path of how to deal with your body, mind, sentiments that is helping you to change perception. That is called sadhana. That is the way by which you purify your essentialness.

• Practicing sadhana isn't your run of the mill tendency. Regardless, when you fathom the example of your body – brain and perceive how you keep repeating models and make messes up, around at that point, you endeavor to set up your body-mind unmistakably and move it from its common course.

• Sadhana ousts the internal identity and it pushes toward turning out to be cleaned. Sadhana changes your wavelength from gross to honest. In yoga, each preparation is to purify your whole system. Your nadis become clear, and greater imperativeness travels through.

• Sw. Sivananda says it is basic to sterilize our contemplations. How to do this? One of the practices is satsanga, when you go to the people who ability to think and you listen to them then you consider what they said. The plausibility of sterilization is we are unadulterated soul unadulterated Self.

- Everything about us is exuding unadulterated essentialness. We have tremendous proportion of prana or imperativeness and the guideline is the significant essentialness. We have it in abundance. Everything else we do is just to clean the covering that is discouraging that splendor of the Self that is starting at now inside us. The more you increment Self-data or Self-care the greater essentialness or prana you get.

CPSIA information can be obtained
at www.ICGtesting.com
Printed in the USA
LVHW081752101221
705864LV00002B/367